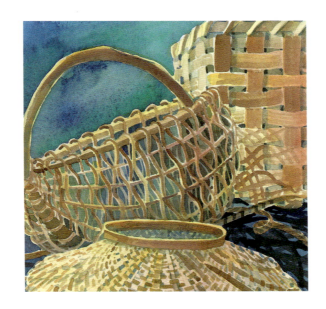

A
is for
Appalachia!

The Alphabet Book of Appalachian Heritage

Written by
Linda Hager Pack

Illustrated by
Pat Banks

THE UNIVERSITY PRESS OF KENTUCKY

Published by The University Press of Kentucky
Scholarly publisher for the Commonwealth,
serving Bellarmine University, Berea College, Centre
College of Kentucky, Eastern Kentucky University,
The Filson Historical Society, Georgetown College,
Kentucky Historical Society, Kentucky State University,
Morehead State University, Murray State University,
Northern Kentucky University, Transylvania University,
University of Kentucky, University of Louisville,
and Western Kentucky University.
All rights reserved.

Editorial and Sales Offices: The University Press of Kentucky
663 South Limestone Street, Lexington, Kentucky 40508-4008
www.kentuckypress.com

13 12 11 10 09   1 2 3 4 5

Library of Congress Cataloging-in-Publication Data

Pack, Linda Hager.
A is for Appalachia : the alphabet book of Appalachian heritage /
written by Linda Hager Pack ; illustrated by Pat Banks.
p. cm.
Previously published: 2nd ed. Prospect, Ky. :
Harmony House Publishers, 2003.
Summary: An alphabet book featuring words about Appalachian culture,
plus additional stories and facts, a glossary, and a list of places to
visit in the region.
ISBN 978-0-8131-2556-5 (hardcover : alk. paper)
1. Appalachian Region, Southern—Social life and customs—Juvenile
literature. 2. Alphabet books—Juvenile literature. I. Banks, Pat, ill. II. Title.
F217.A65P33 2009
975—dc22

2009023104

This book is printed on acid-free paper meeting
the requirements of the American National Standard
for Permanence in Paper for Printed Library Materials.

Printed in China.
Everbest Printing Co.
334 Huanshi Road South
Nansha, Panyu
China 511458
Date of production: May 27, 2009
Cohort: Batch 1

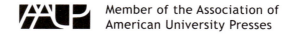

Member of the Association of
American University Presses

With much love and appreciation,
I dedicate this book

to Uncle Bill (Dr. William Plumley) for sharing
with me his love, his appreciation for "things
Appalachian," and his passion for writing;

to Jim and Robin, my husband and
daughter, for their much-needed company
and patient support during my many
research trips;

to my parents, Bob and Oberita Hager, for
loving me so "very good" and for
giving me time to write;

to Josh, my son, for the courage he
demonstrated in editing and critiquing
my writing;

and to Elizabeth Leigh, my granddaughter,
for giving me such joy!

You light my life and delight my heart,

L. H. P.

Introduction

The Appalachia that I know and love is in the Southern Appalachian Mountains. I grew up there, in the small town of Hamlin, West Virginia. Childhood memories of barefoot mornings, blackberry picking, and the annual church Christmas programs will forever fuel my affection for the people and the place.

The Appalachia about which I write is of a distant time and place. It is populated with strong people whose ancestors came primarily from Scotland, Ireland, England, and Germany. When our country was young and under English rule, it was our Appalachian ancestors who resisted being governed or taxed by England. Being fiercely independent, they moved west into the mountains where they joined the proud people of the Cherokee Nation. They lived in log homes, grew their own food, made their own clothes, and crafted their own tools. They told haint tales by the evening fire and Jack tales while at work during the day. They sang sad ballads on front porches and danced to lively jigs played on homemade fiddles and banjos. They worked hard, rested little, and took pride in a job well done. They cared about each other and about their mountains, and they gave thanks to their God. It is this rich heritage that I joyfully share with you.

Linda Hager Pack

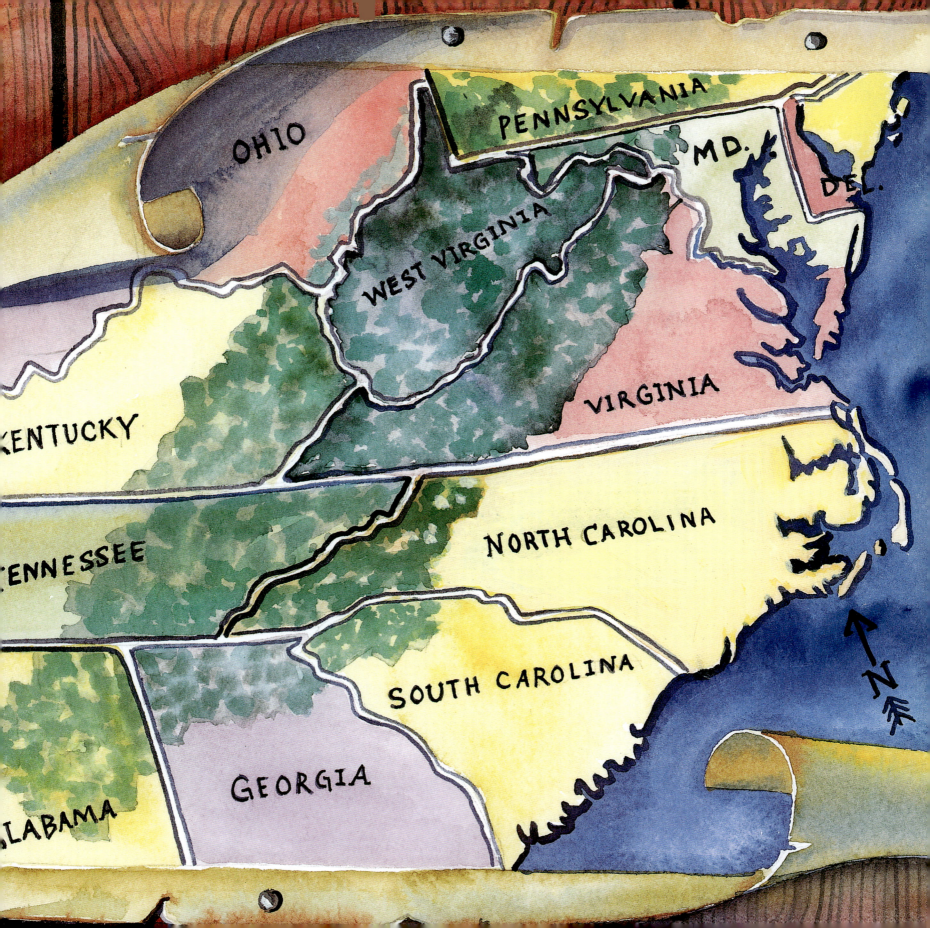

Aa

is for Appalachia!

Appalachia can be defined as a place, a people, and a way of life. The place known as Appalachia is the Appalachian Mountains. It is an ancient land, perhaps over half a billion years old. It is rich with clear mountain streams, thick forests, deep valleys, and the tradition of the people who settled there.

The spine of these mountains rises up across the eastern United States from New York to Alabama, but in this book we will visit only the area known as the Southern Appalachian Mountains. The shaded area on the previous map shows that the Southern Appalachian Mountains span the entire state of West Virginia, eastern Kentucky, southeast Ohio, southwestern Virginia, eastern Tennessee, western North Carolina, a few counties in South Carolina, northern Georgia, and down through northern Alabama.

Bb

is for baskets. Created by hand and fashioned by wit, the basket was as beautiful as it was useful. If something needed to be carried, gathered, or stored, there was a basket for the job. Probably the most popular use for a basket was gathering and marketing eggs. Baskets were sturdy and made to last, so most basketmakers preferred weaving their baskets with splits made from white oak trees. A well-made basket could be used for over a hundred years!

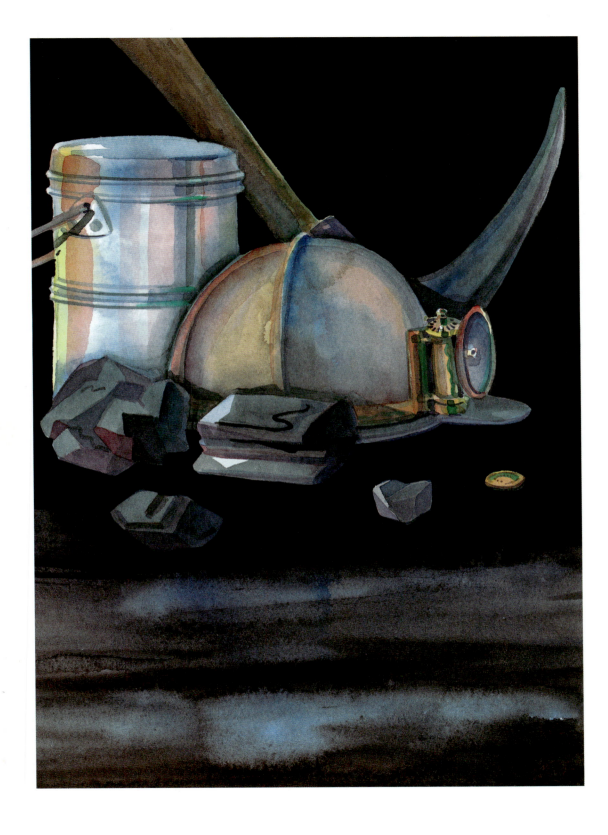

Cc

is for coal. Appalachians used coal to heat their homes and to stoke their cooking fires. Blacksmiths used coal to fuel the hot fires they needed to forge iron and steel into tools and cooking utensils. Some mountain folk made a living by mining coal from deep inside the earth. The work was hard and dangerous, and the miners toiled long hours using picks and shovels. Miners wore lighted hats to help them see in the black darkness of the mines and they carried their lunches in silver lunch buckets. Instead of money, coal companies paid the miners with scrip that could only be spent at the **company store**.

Definitions for words in bold print are found in the glossary on page 42.

Cc

is also for corn. Corn was the main crop in the mountains, and every part of the plant was put to good use. Farmers stored their harvested corn in corn cribs and they took their best ears to **gristmills** where it was ground into cornmeal. Corn could be eaten several ways: fresh on the cob, as hominy and grits (a cereal), and in cornbread. The fodder (leaves) was used to feed animals; the cobs were used to stuff mattresses; and the shucks could be used to make dolls, hats, mops, mats, and bottoms for chairs. Corn also provided a "good time" when neighbors were invited over for a corn shuckin'. (You'll find out more about that on the Hh page.)

Dd

is for dulcimer. Now there's an instrument of which to be proud! Even its name means "sweet music." The dulcimer has been in the Appalachian Mountains for a very long time, and many of the "old timers" called it "dulcymore" or "delcymore." The dulcimer was held on the lap and used to accompany ballads and hymns (but not in church). We like to think of it as an American instrument; but a similar instrument, the scheitholt, originated in Germany where many of our **ancestors** lived.

You won't find a picture of a fiddle on this page. No, Sir! Churchgoing people considered it to be the "devil's box"!

Don't be looking at this page, youngun'! It's that old "devil's box" that the churches preached against! (You see, the fiddle was used to play fast music that made young people want to just stomp their feet and dance. Sometimes they'd stay out dancing on Saturday nights and not get up for church on Sunday mornings! That could only be the devil's doing!)

Ee

Mountain speech was colorful and very functional.

"You air eatin' your yaller corn bread."
(Having the best time of your life.)

Mountain people sprinkled their words with r's.

Window was *winder*.
Tomorrow was *tomorrer*.
Narrow was *narrer*.
Wash was *warsh*.
Ruined was *rurnt*.
Potato was *tater*.
Hush was *hursh*.
Widow was *widder*.

Appalachians didn't pronounce the "g" in endings.

Coming was *a-com'n*.
Reading was *a-read'n*.
Fighting was *a-fight'n*.
Spelling was *a-spellin'*.
Singing was *a-singin'*.
Writing was *a-writin'*.

is for the expressions Appalachians used. Visitors to the mountains often thought that Appalachians talked funny. Mountain people sprinkled their words with r's: window became winder and yellow became yaller They stuck an "a" in front of verbs and dropped the "g" in endings: fighting was a-fightin'; spelling was a-spellin'; and guess what reading was. Instead of saying that a picture hung crooked, they said that it was a-hangin' catawompus. These colorful expressions actually date back to the old English spoken during the 1600's by our Scotch-Irish ancestors. When they came to America and migrated to the back country of the mountains, they carried their speech with them. And there it has stayed.

Ff

is for the farmstead. The early Appalachian people built their homes with the materials that nature provided: logs and stones. The home was the center of family life, but it took much more than a house to survive life in the rugged mountains. A woodshed sat near the house to protect the wood used for heating and cooking. A pigpen sheltered the pigs that provided the main source of meat for the family. A **springhouse** protected the family's water source and acted as a "natural refrigerator" for keeping food cool.

A corn crib stored the harvested corn that was so essential to the family's diet. A meat house was used for preserving and storing meat. A bee-gum stand (a group of hollow black gum logs) housed colonies of bees that made the honey needed for sweetening. A barn was built to safeguard livestock, hay, farming equipment, and tools. A sorghum mill was pulled by an ox or horse to squeeze the juice from sugar cane to make sorghum molasses also used for sweetening. All of this, and we still haven't talked about the garden!

Gg

is for ghost stories. (You like this page already, don't you?) The woods are dark in the mountains, and the shadows of trees hold mysterious tales of **boogers and haints**. Lurking in the darkness of the cemeteries and forests, the haints made themselves known to the Appalachians as balls of fire and shadowy figures that floated above the ground. Like most children, mountain younguns enjoyed sitting by a fire or a kerosene lamp and being frightened by the telling of haint tales. Some believed the stories about boogers and haints, but most folks just had a good time sharing the tales that had been passed down for generations in their families.

Pssst... If you feel real brave, read the story on this page!

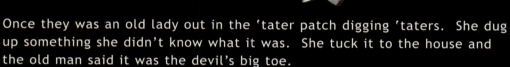

A Ghost Story

"The Devil's Big Toe"

Once they was an old lady out in the 'tater patch digging 'taters. She dug up something she didn't know what it was. She tuck it to the house and the old man said it was the devil's big toe.

Well, she cooked that big toe and eat it. Then along in the night they was laying in the bed, and they heared a voice, said, "Where's my big toe?"

She said, "Jump up, old man, and look in the cellar and out-a-doors!"

The old man he got up and looked under the cellar and out-a-doors and he couldn't see nothing. He laid back down. The voice come again,
"Where's my big toe?"

"Jump up, old man, and look under the bed and up in the loft."

He got up and he looked under the bed and up in the loft and he never seen nothing. He laid back down. The voice come again,
"Where's my big toe?"

"Get up, old lady, and look under the bed and up in the loft and up in the chimley."

She got up and she looked under the bed and up in the loft and up in the chimley and there it set. She said, "What's them big eyes for?"

It said, "To see you, madam!"

"What's them big ears for?"

"To hear you, madam."

"What's that big nose for?"

"To smell you, madam."

"What's that big beard for?"

"To sweep down your chimley."

"What's them big claws for?"

"To tear you all to pieces."

He jumped down on the old lady and tore her all to pieces for eating his big toe.

* Taken from Sang Branch Settlers: Folksongs and Tales of a Kentucky Mountain Family by Leonard Roberts. Permission given by his wife, Edith Roberts.

Hh

is for happenings.

"Working hours" were from sunup to sundown, but work wasn't all that happened in the mountains. Or was it? Families took Sundays off to go to church meetin's with all-day singin' and eatin' on the grounds. They also got together for bean stringin's, candy breakin's, molasses makin', hog killin's, peathrashin's, candy pullin's, and pie suppers at school. Perhaps the most fun they had was at a corn shuckin'! A man would "send the word out" when he was ready to shuck his corn, and the neighbors would come in to help. The neighbors would shuck corn until dinner time when they would sit down to a huge feast prepared by the women in the host family. The teenagers looked forward to corn shuckings because any boy who found a red ear of corn got to kiss the girl of his choice!

Ii

is for iron. Iron was essential in the lives of the early Appalachians. It was forged by the blacksmith to make tools, guns, cooking utensils, hinges, chains, hooks, nails, and barrel hoops. The blacksmith forged the iron by heating it and then hammering it into the form he needed. He made repairs using the same method because nothing was ever thrown away in the mountains. The blacksmith's skill made him a very valuable member of the mountain community.

Jj

is for the clever boy in the Jack Tales. Perhaps you've rocked in a chair, sat on a lap, or snuggled in a bed while someone read to you or told you a story. Do you remember hanging on every word, eager to know the ending but not wanting it to end? Mountain children loved stories, too. Adults soon learned that one sure-fire way to keep younguns "on the job" was to tell them a story. A favorite story hero was a brave boy named Jack. Jack had two brothers, Tom and Will, and he was ALWAYS outsmarting a giant in his stories. But best of all, Jack was a country boy just like the children who loved hearing about him.

But remember, that these tales were TOLD and not read.

"Jack and The Bean Stalk"

Once upon a time there was a mother and her son Jack living in wealth. One night a great giant come to their house and took from them a bag of gold, their magic harp and their little hen that laid golden eggs. They never had a thing left but an old brown cow.

One morning his mother sent Jack to market to trade the old brown cow for some grub. About dusty dark that evening Jack come back home. His mother was uneasy about Jack because there wa'nt no food in the house and she was hungry. When she saw Jack a-comin' she run out to the paling fence to meet him. "Well, Jack, what did you get in trade for the old brown cow?"

Jack says:
I traded my cow for a little red calf
And in that trade I just lost half;
I traded my calf for a little pink pig,
It wa'n't worth much 'cause it wa'n't very big;
I traded my pig for a little white mouse,
He wouldn't say please and he wouldn't keep house;
So I traded my mouse for a little white bean,
The purtiest bean you ever seen.

Jack's mother flew so mad she throwed the little white bean out the winder into the yard.

Next morning when Jack looked out the winder he saw a great big bean stalk growing in the yard, stretching up and up into the sky as far as he could see. Jack begin to climb the bean stalk while his mother was gone to the woods to see if she could find something for them to eat. He climbed and climbed and climbed until he come to the top of the bean stalk. He saw such a tall building he decided it must be a giant's land up there. Jack walked up to his giant's castle and knocked on the door. As soon as the door come open Jack knowed it was a giant's house for an old woman was looking out at him. Jack said, "Good morning, old woman. My name is Jack."

Old woman said, "Jack, you are a brave boy to come here," and she listened for a minute. Then she whispered softly, "Jack, hide in this kettle right now! I hear the giant a-comin'."

In come the old giant and begin to say:

> *Fee, fie, foe, fum,*
> *1,2,3, and here I come;*
> *Fum, foe, fie, fee,*
> *Here I come, 1,2,3;*
> *Bring my little hem*
> *That lays the golden egg.*

The old woman brought the little hen and it begin to sing:
> Cack, cack-a-dack,
> Cack, cack-a-dack,

When the hen sung awhile the giant went to sleep. Jack slipped out of the kettle and grabbed the little hen and away he run. The little hen knowed Jack and she begun to sing for him. This waked up the old giant and he took down the road after Jack. But Jack clim down the bean stalk and run in home. Run in the door and said, "Look, Mommy, I brought back the little hen that the giant stole from us." The hen begin to sing for the mother.

While the mother was talking to the little hem, Jack clim back up the bean stalk. When the old woman saw him at the door again she said, "Law, Jack, the giant is mad and hunting all over the place for you. I hear him coming now. Here, hide in the kettle quick.!"

Jack just got in the kettle when he heard the giant"

> *Fee, fie, foe, fum*
> *1,2,3, and here I come;*
> *Fum foe, fie, fee,*
> *Here I come, 1,2,3;*
> *Bring me my magic harp.*

The old woman brought the harp and it begin to sing:

> *Harper, harper, where are you?*
> *Come and play a tune or two,*
> *In the summer or in the spring*
> *Play the strings and I will sing.*

As the harp sung and played the giant fell asleep.

Jack eased out of the kettle and grabbed the harp and away he went. The harp was so happy it begin to sing louder. This woke the giant up and he begin to chase Jack. Jack clim down the bean stalk and run to his mother and said, "Look, Mommy, I brought back the golden harp the giant stole from us." The harp and the little hen were so glad to be home they both sung together.

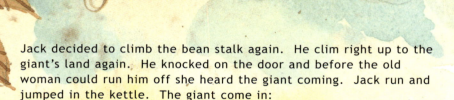

Jack decided to climb the bean stalk again. He clim right up to the giant's land again. He knocked on the door and before the old woman could run him off she heard the giant coming. Jack run and jumped in the kettle. The giant come in:

> *Fee, fie, foe, fum,*
> *1,2,3, and here I come;*
> *Fum, foe, fie, fee,*
> *Here I come, 1,2,3;*

The old woman brought him his money bag. Giant said:

> *Money, money sing to me.*

The Money sung out:

> *Diamonds, rubies, emeralds too*
> *Sparking the silver dew,*
> *Counting them over one by one*
> *Sparkling like the sun.*

This made the giant go to sleep. As soon as Jack heard him snoring he jumped out of the kettle and grabbed the money bag off the table and took off. The money bag begin to sing louder and this woke the old giant. He was so mad at Jack he aimed to kill him and eat him this time. He was going to foller Jack home. Jack hi the bean stalk and clim faster than he ever done before but the giant was gaining on him. When he got down near the earth he dropped the money bag so's he could climb faster. Before he retch the ground his mother sawed the giant down. It fell with a big crash. The giant hit the ground so hard he bounced back up into giant land. They never saw him again, and Jack and his mother lived happily ever after.

Taken from *Old Greasybeard: Tales from the Cumberland Gap* collected and annotated by Leonard Roberts

Kk

is for knife. A mountain man didn't consider himself properly dressed unless he was carrying his pocketknife. If the knife was a Russell's Barlow, then that was even better! With knife in hand and using his imagination, he could whittle something out of just about any piece of wood. There wasn't money to buy toys, puzzles, and gadgets, so it just came naturally to use the knife to shape them. And **whittlin'** was a good way to keep busy while a person caught up on the latest news from his neighbors.

Ll

is for letter edged in black. There was only one thing that could halt all activity in the mountains: a death. The death was announced to neighbors with the tolling of a bell. The haunting sound of the first ring told them to listen; then the bell tolled one time for each year the person had lived. People living outside the mountains were given the news of a death in a letter edged in black. This song explains the sorrow a man feels when he receives such a letter in an envelope that is also edged in black.

The Letter Edged in Black

I was standing by my window yesterday morning,
Without a tho't of sorrow or of care;
When I saw the postman coming up the pathway,
With such a smiling face and jolly air.

He rang the bell, then whistled as he waited,
And then he said "good morning to you, Jack",
But he little knew the sorrow that he bro't me,
When he handed me the letter edged in black.

With trembling hands I took the letter from him,
I opened it and this is what it said:
" Come home, my boy, your dear old daddy needs you,
Come home, my boy, your dear old mother's dead.

The last words that your mother ever uttered,
Were 'Tell my boy I want him to come back';
My eyes are blurred, my poor old heart is breaking,
As I'm writing you this letter edged in black."

Mm

is for mountain music!
Music kept the beat of life's
rhythm in the mountains. Morning,
noon, and night, there was music.
Ballads could be heard in the
fields as farmers hoed or by
the evening fires where families
gathered after supper. A mother's
voice sang lullabies to her
children, and congregations lifted
up hymns to their Lord on Sunday
mornings. Lively songs and dance
jigs were played on fiddles and
banjos while couples danced in
barns or in the large rooms of
houses where the furniture
had been broken down (moved
outside). There were even singing
schools held at the one-room
schools where adults learned to
read **shaped notes** so they could
sing hymns in four-part harmony.

Cherokee Syllabary

CWY ᎠᏍᎦᏯ ᏗᎪᏪᎵ (stylized title)

D a	R e	T i	Ꭳ o	Ꭴ u	i
Ꭶ ga Ꭺ ka	Ꭸ ge	Ꭹ gi	Ꭺ go	Ꭻ gu	Ꭼ gv
Ꭵ ha	Ꭾ he	Ꭿ hi	Ꮀ ho	Ꮁ hu	Ꮂ hv
W la	Ꮄ le	Ꮅ li	Ꮆ lo	Ꮇ lu	Ꮈ lv
Ꮉ ma	Ꮊ me	Ꮋ mi	Ꮌ mo	Ꮍ mu	
Ꮎ na Ꮟ hna Ꮐ nah	Ꮑ ne	Ꮒ ni	Ꮓ no	Ꮔ nu	Ꮕ nv
Ꮖ qwa	Ꮗ qwe	Ꮘ qwi	Ꮙ qwo	Ꮚ qwu	Ꮛ qwv
Ꮜ sa Ꮝ s	Ꮞ se	Ꮟ si	Ꮠ so	Ꮡ su	Ꮢ sv
Ꮣ da Ꮤ ta	Ꮥ de Ꮦ te	Ꮧ di Ꮨ ti	Ꮩ do	Ꮪ du	Ꮫ dv
Ꮬ dla Ꮭ tla	Ꮮ tle	Ꮯ tli	Ꮰ tlo	Ꮱ tlu	Ꮲ tlv
Ꮳ tsa	Ꮴ tse	Ꮵ tsi	Ꮶ tso	Ꮷ tsu	Ꮸ tsv
Ꮹ wa	Ꮺ we	Ꮻ wi	Ꮼ wo	Ꮽ wu	Ꮾ wv
Ꮿ ya	Ᏸ ye	Ᏹ yi	Ᏺ yo	Ᏻ yu	Ᏼ yv

There was a great Cherokee named Sequoyah who became very interested in the white settlers' **"talking leaf."** He worked twelve years to invent a Cherokee alphabet that allowed his people to read and write the Cherokee language. They were soon publishing their own newspaper.

THANKS SUN or MOON MOUNTAIN  CORN

Nn

is for Native Appalachians.
The first people to settle in the Appalachian Mountains were the Ani-Yun'wiya, the Principal People. We know them today as the Cherokee. Their ancestors walked across a land bridge from Asia thousands of years before Columbus made his journey to America. The Cherokee were farmers and their main crops were the "three sisters": corn, beans, and squash. The women did the farming and gathered berries, nuts, and wild plants from the forests with their children. They made clothing from tanned deerskin using needles made from bone. The men fished; they hunted deer, turkey, and bears; they fought enemies; and they traded with "outsiders."

The Cherokee lived in villages near rivers, and each village had families from the seven different Cherokee clans: Bird, Paint, Deer, Wolf, Blue, Long Hair, and Wild Potato. A village might have as many as forty to sixty dwellings with a Council House located in the center. It was in the Council House that government meetings, celebrations, and religious ceremonies were held.

Oo

is for the one-room school.
School in the mountains began at
the end of harvest and ended in
time for spring planting. Students
were often called "scholars."
They walked as far as four miles
to school, often barefoot, where
they learned the **3R's** and their
a-b-abs. The weekly **spelling bee**
was a favorite activity and adults
often came to school on Fridays to
join in the competition.

Children carried their lunches in
hand-woven oak baskets or silver
lard buckets with tight-fitting lids.
The baskets and buckets were
placed on a high shelf in the back
of the room and inside were lunches of sweet milk and cornbread,
biscuits and honey, leftovers from
breakfast or supper the night
before, or maybe even a hammer
and walnuts to crack.

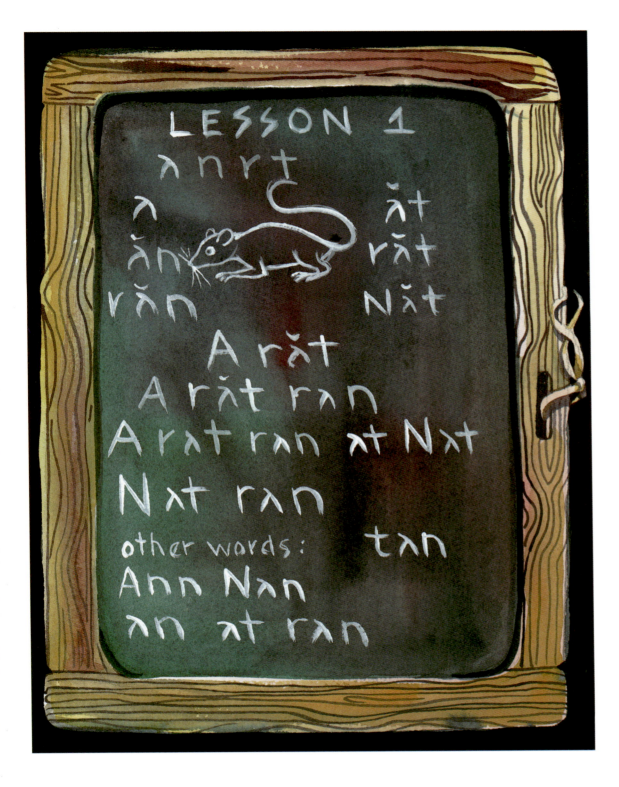

Scholars sat on wooden benches and held black slates in their laps for writing and figuring. Boys sat on the right side of the classroom and girls sat on the left. Younger children sat in the front of the room and older children sat in the back. The students were warmed by a potbellied stove that sat in the center of the room, and they sometimes spent recess cutting and gathering wood to burn in it. They drank water from a wooden bucket where they shared a gourd dipper. They took care of personal business in outhouses located on either side of the school: one for boys and one for girls.

We can't forget the box or pie suppers held at school. What fun! The teacher would organize one of these events when she needed to make some money for the school. This is the way it worked: each girl would make a supper (or a pie if it was a pie supper) and put it in a box she decorated real pretty. The boys would bid on the boxes hoping they would get the supper made by the girl they liked. Now this is the tricky part: no one knew which girl cooked which box supper! So a boy might bid on a box because it was real pretty and not get to eat the dinner his girlfriend cooked. That meant that he didn't get to eat with his girlfriend, either!

Pp

is for the people in the Appalachian Mountains. The people who settled in the Appalachian Mountains were largely a mixture of Native Americans from the Cherokee Tribe and immigrants who had come to this country from Scotland, Ireland, Germany, and England. They were a proud people who shared with their children the customs, stories, and language of their "grands and greats" (ancestors). They grew their own food, made their own clothes, forged their own tools, and built their own homes from the materials provided by Mother Nature. Life was hard and the work unending, but these strong people still made the time to celebrate life in their music, their worship, and their social gatherings. Those of us who have grown up in Appalachia can count ourselves fortunate.

"I reckon at jist a-bout ever'thang's a heap better when yer a-livin' in the mountains."

Qq

is for quilts (sometimes known as bed kivers). Quilts were made for the practical purpose of keeping the early settlers warm, but mountain women had a talent for taking scraps of fabric and turning them into beautiful works of art. The women enjoyed gathering at a home for a quilting bee. They often sounded like a hive of busy bees as they sat around a large quilting frame stitching and catching up on the local gossip. They designed and named many quilt patterns which they enjoyed trading like recipes. The "friendship quilt" was a favorite because each woman at the quiltin' embroidered her name on a square she had quilted.

Rr

is for a-raisin'. And it isn't the kind you eat! No, sir! A mountain raisin' was a gathering of families to raise (build) a house or a barn and sometimes even a school. Trees were cut and logs were hauled in on sleds pulled by mules or oxen. Everyone worked! The women and girls prepared the food and sometimes had a quiltin' bee. Young boys carried water and laid out tools for the men. The men brought tools which they used to split and notch logs, smooth boards, and lay the cabin floors. Fifteen to twenty men could raise the walls, lay the floor, and roof a house in just a few days. Then it was time to eat, listen to good music, and dance!

Ss

is for spinning and weaving.
The spinning wheel and the loom were used by women to make clothing and **kivers** for their families. Wool was sheared from sheep in the spring of the year, and then it was washed and **carded** into soft, fluffy rolls ready for spinning. Using the spinning wheel, the mountain mother spun the wool into yarn. If she desired a color, she would dye the yarn. Walnut hulls were used to make dark brown, yellow-root was used to make orange, green oak leaves were used to make green, and pokeberries were used to make red. The thread or yarn could then be used to weave cloth on a loom or it could be used to knit socks, stockings, gloves, hats, and sweaters for the family. Nothing could keep the feet warmer than a good pair of wool socks.

Tt

is for toys! Of course!
Batteries weren't included or
needed in Appalachian toys. Boys
were partial to carrying slingshots,
pocket knives, and blowguns. Girls
enjoyed dolls made from apples,
potatoes, sticks, rocks, corncobs,
cornshucks, and rags. Marbles
were molded from colored clay,
young tree saplings became
walking stilts, and an old button
on a string could make a marvelous
noise. All that was needed was
a good imagination and a little
help from Mother Nature.

Uu

is for the undertaker.
Cemeteries dot the hillsides and churchyards of the Appalachian Mountains, reminding us that death was very much a part of Appalachian life. Within hours of the eerie ring of the tolling bell, the undertaker began the lonesome job of building a casket for the person who had died. He worked quickly while older women in the community busied themselves with the task of **laying out the body**. Neighbors brought food, helped dig the grave, and joined the grieving family in sitting up all night with the body. Although the burial took place right away, funerals were usually preached in the spring when the **circuit rider**, a preacher, made his ride through the mountain communities.

Vv

is for vegetable garden

or "sass patch" as it was called by the early settlers. The garden was planted close to the house and tended by the women. It was surrounded by a fence to protect it from the animals that were allowed to roam free to graze. Most gardens consisted of green beans, corn, beets, cabbage, carrots, turnips, okra, onions, sweet potatoes, Irish potatoes, pumpkins, squash, tomatoes, rutabagas, parsnips, and garden greens such as lettuce, collard and mustard. Beans were a favorite vegetable. They were strung by needle on a thread and hung to dry so they could be eaten in cold weather. These dried beans were called "leather breeches," and they were often seen hanging on fireplaces and from rafters in the home.

Ww

is for water. Water was nature's ultimate gift to the early settlers and their much-loved mountains. Sometimes roaring, sometimes gurgling, mountain water was always cool and clear. It quenched the settlers' thirst, watered their crops, powered their grist mills, cooled their food in springhouses, and determined where they would build their homes. Many of the "old timers" complained loudly about the awful taste of "city water" when they visited town. They preferred to drink the fresh water from their mountain springs.

is for Xmas (Christmas).

Christmas in the mountains was heartfelt, homemade, and gathered from the skirts of Mother Nature. Churches and houses were filled with the outdoor aroma of pine, cedar, holly, and mistletoe. Christmas trees were cut from the forest and decorated with strings of homegrown popcorn and berries, garlands of cutout paper dolls and angels, bows made from strips of fabric, stars covered with foil that had been saved all year, and chains made from strips of paper cut from Sears Roebuck catalogs. Women busied themselves with baking, and the air was charged with smells of gingerbread, apple stack cakes, molasses cookies, turkey, and ham. And before going to bed on Christmas Eve, children excitedly hung their stockings in the hope that Santa would fill them with apples, stick candy, oranges, and an occasional handmade doll or carved wooden toy.

Early Christians used the χ as a symbol to represent their Christian identity.

Yy

is for yarb doctor. There were a few "book" doctors in the mountain areas, but most people relied on nature's own medicine to soothe their pain and cure their ills. "Yarb" was a mountain word for herb, and a yarb doctor was someone who was skilled in using herbs and plants to heal. The yarb doctor used all the parts of a plant to stock his private pharmacy. Roots were beaten to make poultices (salves) to spread on sores and draw out infection. Leaves, roots, and bark were dried and powdered to make teas that often needed to be sweetened in order to drink. Many of the remedies sound "odd" to us today, but people would travel a great distance to seek the advice of a truly skilled yarb doctor.

Examples of Remedies

Bleeding:
Place a spider web across the wound.
Use pine resin.

Colds:
Chew the leaves and stems of peppermint.
Put Ginger and sugar in hot water.
Drink and go to bed.
Drink tea from the roots of butterfly weed.
Eat onions roasted in ashes.
Put goose-grease salve on chest.
Drink tea made from wintergreen fern.
Boil pine needles to make a strong tea.

Earache:
Roast cabbage stalks and squeeze the juice into ear. Blow smoke from rabbit tobacco in the ear.

Fever:
A tea made of rabbit tobacco will break a fever.

Zz

is for zodiac. The zodiac forms an imaginary band in the heavens, and it is divided equally into twelve constellations of stars: Aries, Taurus, Cancer, Virgo, Scorpio, Capricorn, Pisces, Aquarius, Sagittarius, Libra, Leo, and Gemini. As the moon circles the Earth every 29 1/2 days, it passes through each of the zodiac signs. Mountain farmers believed that the moon's phases and its place in the zodiac affected activities here on Earth. Using *The Farmer's Almanac* to determine the phase of the moon and its place in the zodiac, the farmers cleared their fields, built their homes, planted their seeds, and harvested their crops "by the sign." If there was a job to be done, there was a sign in which to do it.

Glossary

a-b-abs was another way to say "alphabet".

ancestors are all of our relatives who lived before us.

boogers and haints were mountain words for ghosts.

cards had handles and strong teeth very much like a pet brush. A set of cards were used to separate wool fibers so that the wool could be combed into rolls for spinning. The top card was filled with raw wool, and then it was drawn over the bottom card using a firm stroke for about ten or twelve times. The wool was again placed on the top card and the process repeated until the wool was soft and fluffy.

Cherokee clans were groupings of people who were related or descended from the same ancestors. There were seven clans and members of a clan were considered to be blood brothers and sisters. Men and women had to marry outside their clan. Cherokee children belonged to their mother's clan and it was the mother who did most of the children's training. As boys grew older, the mother's brothers or other men in the clan took on more responsibility in the boy's training. Each clan was represented on the council by a member or counselor. Women had equal say with men about what happened in the tribe.

circuit rider was a preacher who rode a circuit (circular path) on his horse to preach at various mountain churches. He couldn't travel in the mountains during the cold, winter months, so his circuit usually began in the spring of the year when the Sarvis trees began to bloom. He would preach at one church, travel the loop of his other churches preaching, and then he would begin again.

company store was a store owned by a coal company. Just about anything could be bought there. Miners were paid by the coal companies with scrip. The only place that scrip could be spent was at the company's store.

Farmer's Almanac was and is an almanac that is published once a year. The magazine includes planting calendars, advice, remedies, and advertisements. It predicts the weather, and it charts the phases of the moon and the moon's path in the zodiac.

grist mill was a mill that used large stones to grind corn into cornmeal. Water was used to make the mill go around and do the grinding. People who had grist mills would grind corn for their neighbors in exchange for some of the cornmeal.

kivers were covers used on beds to keep the mountaineers warm. Quilts were called kivers.

laying out the body involved bathing and dressing a dead body and preparing it for burial. This difficult job was often done by the older women in the community, and sometimes it was done by the preacher if the body was a man. The body was sometimes laid on the kitchen table or sometimes on a bed to complete the bathing and dressing. Coins were often placed on the dead person's eyes to keep them closed during visitation.

shaped notes originated in New England around the eighteenth century when people began having singing schools to improve their singing in church. Few people could actually read music so shaped notes were used to help people keep the melody of the hymns. Originally there were four shaped notes, and each of the notes had a different shaped head so that people could tell them apart. A song was first sung by pronouncing the notes (fa-la-sol-mi-sol-la); and then the words were sung using the melody of the notes.

spelling bee was a favorite school competition. The students would line up around the classroom. The teacher would give the first child a word to spell. If the child spelled his/her word correctly, he got to stay in the competition; if he/she misspelled the word, she had to sit down and was out of the competition. After receiving a word from the teacher, the child has to 1) say the word; 2) spell the word; 3) say the word. If the student failed to do any one of the three steps he was out of the game. The last student standing was the winner and considered to be the best speller.

springhouse was a small building built near or on a spring. The cool spring water ran through the house where it was kept clean for drinking. Rocks were piled or shelves built inside the building so that food could be kept cool.

3R's were Reading, Writing (silent w), and 'Rithmetic.

talking leaf was how the Cherokee referred to the white man's newspaper.

whittlin' was the simple activity of using a knife to shape a twig or a piece of wood. Sometimes the wood took form, and sometimes slivers were shaved or whittled from it until nothing was left but a small pile of wood shavings.

Acknowledgments

Places

Museum of Appalachia, Norris, Tennessee
Great Smoky Mountains National Park
    GSMNP Archives
    Cades Cove
    Little Greenbrier School
    The Walker Sisters' home
    Farmstead at Cataloochee
    Noah "Bud" Ogle Cabin
    Cable Mill
Hensley Settlement at Cumberland Gap National Historical Park, Kentucky
Mountain Homeplace, Paintsville, Kentucky
National Storytelling Festival, Jonesborough, Tennessee
The Appalachian Museum at Berea College, Berea, Kentucky
Berea College Archives, Berea, Kentucky
Eastern Kentucky University Archives, Richmond, Kentucky

People

Dr. William Plumley, Barbara Patton, Oberita and Bob Hager, and Emmerson Pearson, my family
Pat Banks for her friendship and beautiful illustrations
Mr. and Mrs. Leonard Roberts, who generously allowed me to use a ghost story and Jack tale from Mr. Roberts's collection
Tim Cruze, Latonya Miller, David Carney, David Brown, Brett Painter, Larry Stanton, rangers at Great Smoky Mountains National Park

Miss Elsie Burrell and Robin Goddard at the Little Greenbrier School
D. B. Manning, Charles Hay, Shelby Combs, and Linda Fagan of Richmond, Kentucky
Loyal Jones of Berea, Kentucky
Loretta Hammond, Catherine Smith, Phillip Wood, Julia Jayne, and Brian Cox at the Mountain Homeplace
Matt Graham at the Hensley Settlement
Paul and Bonnie Purcell, Hayden and Winnie Phillippie, and Thelma
Carl Bean and Raye Rutherford at the Museum of Appalachia and Joe Paul Pruett and William Strode, two great guys!

L. H. P.

I appreciate this opportunity to reflect upon the many wonderful people who have enriched my life and work. My father's father taught me how to love the woods, creeks, mountains, caves, and stars. My father's mother taught me how to find and cook wild greens. My mother's father had a country store, and my mother's mother loved flowers of all kinds, especially the "old ones." The illustrations for A is for Appalachia! were inspired by our family.

I believe I had the luck of having been born to the best parents ever! My life mate has been a source of love and unconditional support. My two beautiful sons have inspired and challenged me to be the best I can be. Life is a wonderful journey—especially when it begins in the hills of eastern Kentucky.

P. B.

Want to know more about Appalachia? Visit these places:

Kentucky
- Appalshop Community Arts and Media Center (Whitesburg)
- Brush Arbor Appalachian Homestead (Renfro Valley)
- Coal House Museum (Middlesboro)
- Festival of the Mountain Masters (Harlan)
- Kentucky Coal Mining Museum (Benham)
- Kentucky Folklife Festival (Frankfort)
- Kingdom Come Swappin' Meetin' (Cumberland)
- Loyal Jones Appalachian Center (Berea, folk art capital of Appalachia)
- Mountain Homeplace (Paintsville)
- Van Lear Historical Society Coal Miners' Museum (Van Lear)

North Carolina
- Appalachian Cultural Museum, Appalachian State University (Boone)
- Appalachian Heritage Museum (Blowing Rock)
- Catch the Spirit of Appalachia (grassroots heritage organization; Sylva)
- Cherokee Heritage Museum (Cherokee)
- Hickory Ridge Homestead and Living History Museum (Boone)
- John C. Campbell Folk School (Brasstown)
- Mountain Farm Museum at the Oconaluftee Visitor Center, Great Smoky Mountains National Park (Cherokee)
- Mountain Heritage Center, Western Carolina University (Cullowhee)
- The Mountain Retreat & Learning Center (Highlands)
- Museum of the Cherokee Indian (Cherokee)
- Occaneechi Indian Village (Hillsborough)
- Oconaluftee Indian Village (Cherokee)
- Tobacco Farm Life Museum (Kenly)

Ohio
- Appalachian Gateway Center, Southern State Community College (Sardinia)
- Mountain Days Festival (Dayton)

Tennessee
- Center for Appalachian Studies and Services, East Tennessee State University (Johnson City)
- Cumberland Gap National Historical Park (Cumberland Gap)
- Great Smoky Mountains Institute at Tremont (Townsend)
- Great Smoky Mountains National Park: Cades Cove, Little Greenbrier School, Noah "Bud" Ogle Cabin, Roaring Fork Motor Trail
- Historic Collinsville (Southside)
- Marble Springs State Historic Farmstead (Knoxville)
- McMinn County Living Heritage Museum (Athens)
- Museum of Appalachia (Norris)
- Sequoyah Birthplace Museum (Vonore)

Virginia
- Frontier Culture Museum (Staunton)
- The Homeplace Mountain Farm and Museum (Gate City)
- Thistle Cove Farm (Tazewell)

West Virginia
- Beckley Exhibition Coal Mine (Beckley)
- Heritage Farm Museum and Village (Huntington)
- Youth Museum of Southern West Virginia/Mountain Homestead (Beckley)

About the Author

Linda Hager Pack grew up in the small town of Hamlin, West Virginia, where she was reared by her parents, aunts, uncles, and grandparents to be a proper mountain youngun'. Having determined early on that children are what God does best, Linda decided to become a teacher. She earned her bachelor's and master's degrees in elementary education from Eastern Kentucky University, and in 1996, Kentucky's Governor Paul Patton presented her with the Ashland Oil Teacher Award.

During her twenty-two years of teaching young children in West Virginia and Kentucky, Linda decided to follow the writing advice she often gave her students. She began writing about what she knows and loves: Appalachia.

The author teaches children's literature at Eastern Kentucky University. She has two grown children and a granddaughter, Elleigh. She lives in Richmond with her husband, Jim, and their sad dog, Zoe.

About the Artist

Pat Banks works primarily in watercolor and acrylics. Painting is the lens she uses to explore and interpret the world, especially eastern Kentucky, her home. The beauty of the hills, valleys, and rivers inspires environmental concern as well as artistic expression, and Pat's conservation work focuses mainly on the preservation of Kentucky waterways. Taking time to walk paths in the woods and fields, float down the eternal streams and rivers, and study the "wild things" fosters an appreciation of the preciousness and fragility of this wondrous place.

Pat is a veteran roster artist for the Kentucky Arts Council, an advisor for the Kentucky Peer Advisory Network, a participating artist in the Visual Arts at the Market program, and a member of the Kentucky Guild of Artists and Craftsmen. Her work is exhibited in galleries and other venues throughout the region. She has also served as a visiting artist in Japan, Ecuador, and France.

Pat lives and works in northern Madison County, Kentucky, in a home and studio that she and her husband built. They raise gardens and share their home with several cats and a beautiful yellow Labrador retriever named Cinnamon.